Adventures in Canadian History

The Death of Isaac Brock

Books for Younger Readers by Pierre Berton

The Golden Trail
The Secret World of Og

ADVENTURES IN CANADIAN HISTORY

The Capture of Detroit
The Death of Isaac Brock
Revenge of the Tribes
Canada Under Siege

Bonanza Gold
The Klondike Stampede
Trails of '98
City of Gold
Before the Gold Rush
Kings of the Klondike

Parry of the Arctic
Jane Franklin's Obsession
Dr. Kane of the Arctic Seas
Trapped in the Arctic

The Railway Pathfinders
The Men in Sheepskin Coats
A Prairie Nightmare
Steel Across the Plains

PIERRE BERTON

The Battles of the War of 1812

THE DEATH OF ISAAC BROCK

ILLUSTRATIONS BY SCOTT CAMERON

An M&S Paperback Original from
McClelland & Stewart Inc.
The Canadian Publishers

An M&S Paperback Original from McClelland & Stewart Inc.

First printing April 1991

Reprinted 1993

Canadian Cataloguing in Publication Data

Berton, Pierre, 1920–
The death of Isaac Brock

(Adventures in Canadian history. The battles of the War of 1812)
"An M&S paperback."
Includes index.
ISBN 0-7710-1426-0

1. Brock, Isaac, Sir, 1769–1812 – Juvenile literature. 2. Canada – History – War of 1812 – Biography – Juvenile literature.* 3. Queenston Heights (Ont.), Battle of, 1812 – Juvenile literature. 4. Canada – History – 1791–1841 – Juvenile literature. 5. Generals – Canada – Biography – Juvenile literature. I. Cameron, Scott (Scott R.). II. Title. III. Series: Berton, Pierre, 1920– . Adventures in Canadian history. The battles of the War of 1812.

FC443.B8B47 1991 j971.03'4'092 C91-093137-2
E353.1.B8B47 1991

Series design by Tania Craan
Cover and interior illustrations by Scott Cameron
Maps by James Loates

Typesetting by Pickwick
Printed and bound in Canada

McClelland & Stewart Inc.
The Canadian Publishers
481 University Avenue
Toronto, Ontario
M5G 2E9

Contents

Maps appear on pages viii-ix and page 27

The events in this book actually happened as told here. Nothing has been made up. This is a work of non-fiction and there is archival evidence for every story and, indeed, every remark made in this book.

Adventures in Canadian History

The Death of Isaac Brock

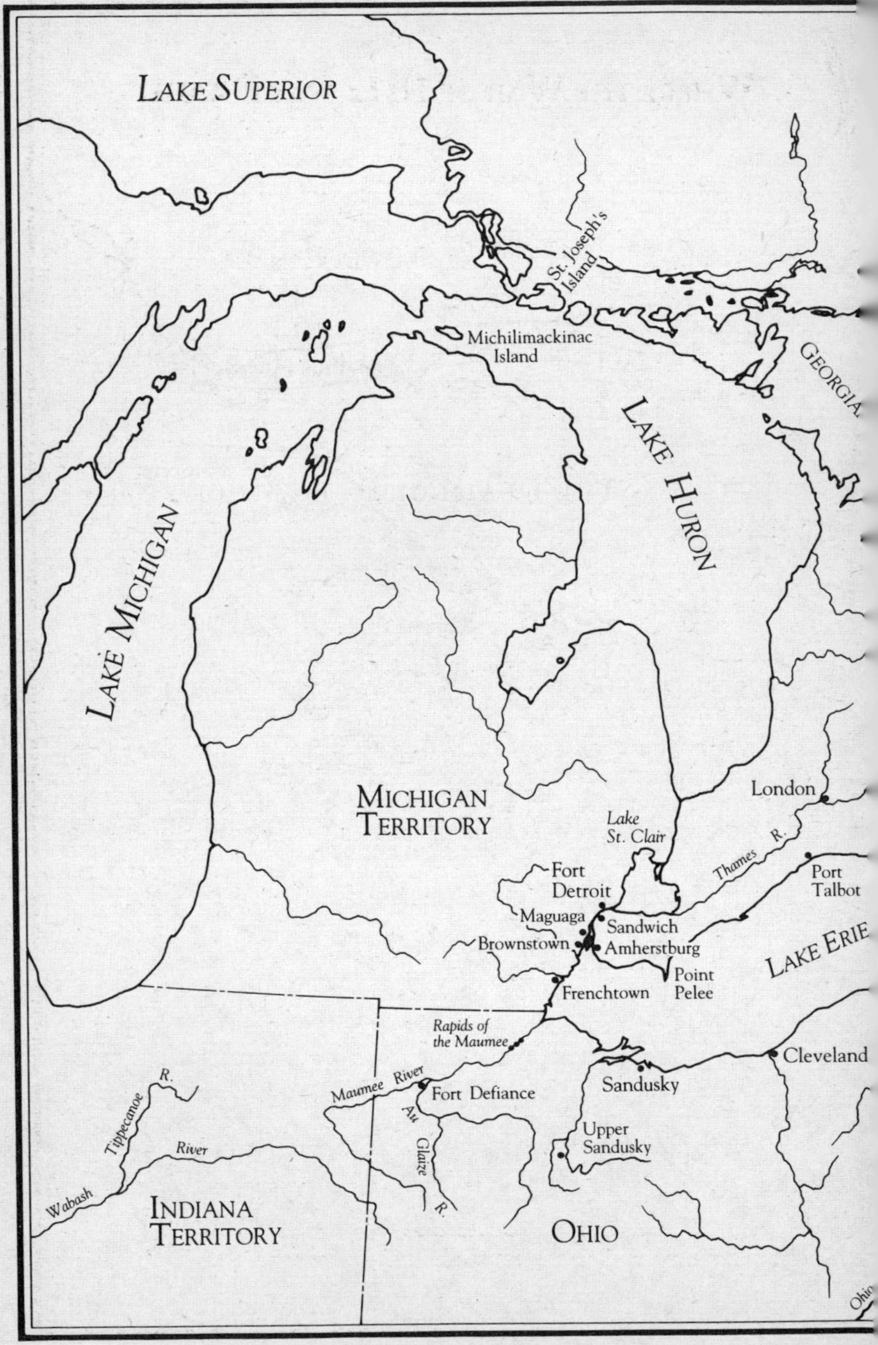

LAKE SUPERIOR
St. Joseph's Island
Michilimackinac Island
GEORGIA
LAKE HURON
LAKE MICHIGAN
MICHIGAN TERRITORY
Lake St. Clair
London
Thames R.
Port Talbot
Fort Detroit
Maguaga
Sandwich
Brownstown
Amherstburg
LAKE ERIE
Point Pelee
Frenchtown
Rapids of the Maumee
Cleveland
Maumee River
Fort Defiance
Sandusky
Au Glaize R.
Upper Sandusky
Tippecanoe R.
River
Wabash
INDIANA TERRITORY
OHIO
Ohio

WHERE THE WAR OF 1812 WAS FOUGHT

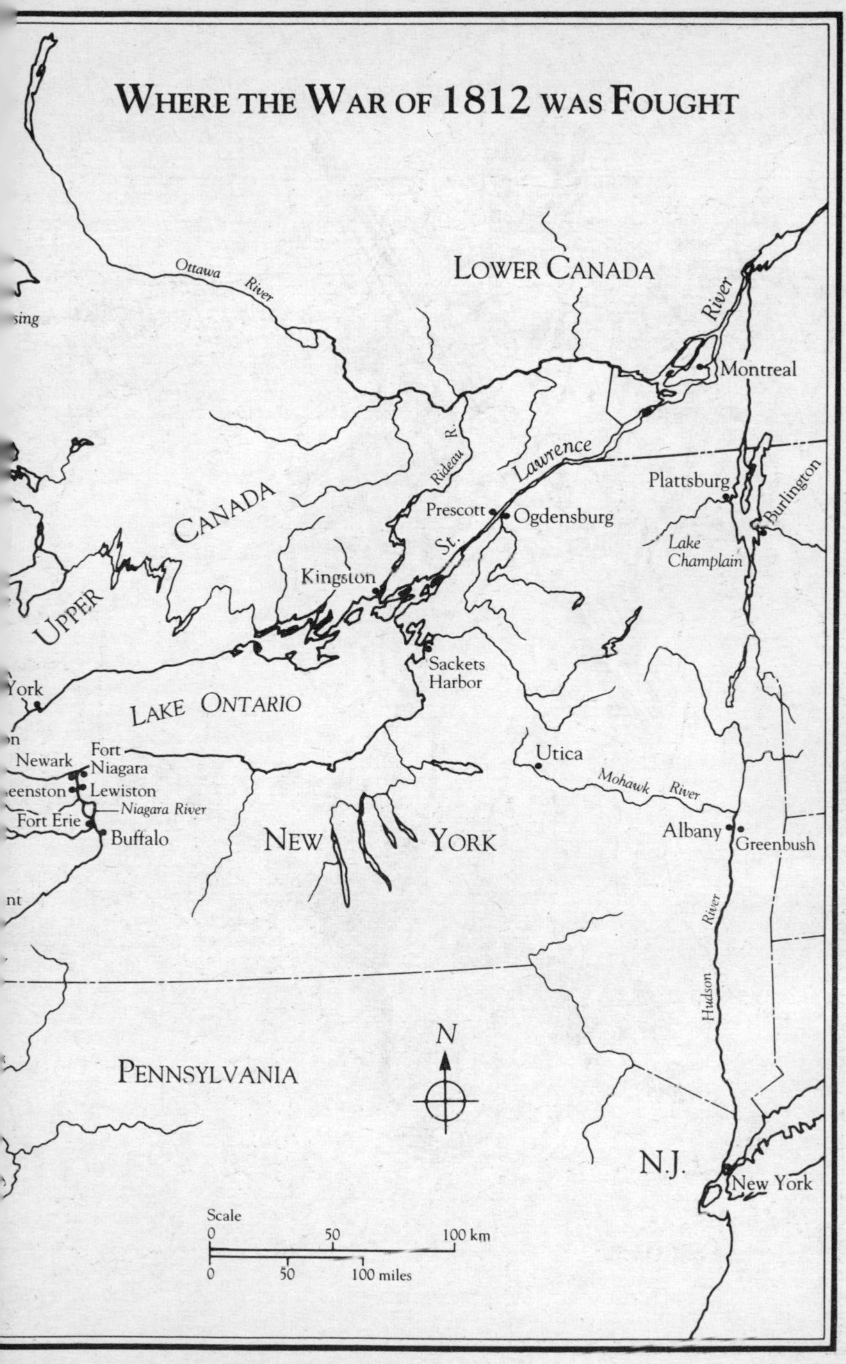

Overview

The peculiar war

When war broke out between the United States and Canada in June of 1812, John Richardson rushed to join the colours. He was only 15 – a slight, curly-headed, clean shaven youth – but, unlike so many of his neighbours, he was eager to serve his country.

Many of his neighbours on the Detroit river were recent arrivals from the United States, reluctant to fight their former compatriots. But Richardson came of solid Canadian stock. His mother's father, John Askin, was a famous fur trader. His grandmother was an Ottawa Indian of the Algonquin nation. And so young John, to his considerable delight, found himself accepted as a "gentleman volunteer" in a regular regiment – the British 41st – stationed in Fort Amherstburg not far from the present site of Windsor. In the next thirty months, he probably saw more of the War of 1812 than any other teenager in Upper Canada.

After fifteen months of fighting, Richardson was captured by the Americans – a capture that tells us a good deal about that most peculiar of wars. Unlike so many prisoners in so many jail cells around the world, he could be fairly sure of decent treatment by his enemies, because he knew so many of them. His grandfather, John Askin, had only to write a note to the American colonel at Fort Detroit asking him to look after the boy. After all, that colonel was Askin's son-in-law. The man in charge of his prison was another relative.

The War of 1812, then, must be seen as a civil war fought by men and women on both sides of a border that all had ignored until hostilities broke out. Many were former neighbours who spoke the same language and were often related to one another. Unlike the Richardsons, three out of every five were former Americans.

Some had come up from the United States after the American Revolution. These "Tories", as their compatriots called them, were fiercely loyal to the British crown. Canadians know them as "United Empire Loyalists". They formed the backbone of the volunteer civilian army, known as the militia.

The others were more recent arrivals. They came to Canada because the land was cheap and taxes almost nonexistent. They wanted to be left alone to clear the land of stumps, to drain the marshes, till the soil, and harvest their crops of wheat, barley and corn, or tend the apple, pear and cherry trees that grew so abundantly along the border.

For them, life was hard enough without war. They built their own cabins and barns with the help of their neighbours and, since there was scarcely anything resembling a shop or a store, they made everything themselves, from farm implements to the homespun clothing that was the universal dress. Those villages that existed at all were mere huddles of shacks. Communication was difficult and sometimes impossible. Newspapers were virtually unknown. In the single room schoolhouses, children learned to read, write, and figure – not much more.

These people didn't want to fight any more than their counterparts, the civilian soldiers south of the border. It was indeed a peculiar war that moved along in fits and starts, like a springless buggy bumping over a dirt track. At harvest time and seeding, farmers on both sides deserted or were sent off to tend to their crops. In winter, nothing moved; it was too cold to fight, and so each autumn all activity was postponed until spring.

It was, like so many conflicts, a very silly war. Communication was so bad that hundreds of soldiers, not to mention generals, had no idea it had begun. The last bloody battle was fought long after peace had been declared. The problems that had caused the war in the first place – Great Britain's attacks on American shipping – were solved well before the war ended. But the war went on – men were maimed and killed, farms were vandalized, barns were burned, whole communities put to the torch, and "traitors" hanged for no purpose.

Why were young Canadians like John Richardson fighting young Americans along the international border? The Canadians who fought did so to protect their country from attack. The Americans were fighting for something less tangible – their honour. Once again, they felt, the British were pushing them around. The War of 1812 was in many ways a continuation of the War of Independence fought forty years before.

It started with Napoleon Bonaparte, the dictator of France. Bonaparte wanted to conquer all of Europe, and so the British found themselves locked in a long and bloody struggle with him – a struggle that began with the great British naval victory at Trafalgar and ended a decade later with the famous battle of Waterloo.

But in their zeal to conquer Napoleon, the British pushed the Americans too far. By boarding American ships on the high seas and kidnapping American sailors for service in the Royal Navy – on the grounds that these seamen were actually British deserters – they got the Americans' backs up. Then, in order to strangle the French by a sea blockade, the British announced they would seize any ship that dared sail directly for a French port. By 1812, they had captured four hundred American vessels, some within sight of the U.S. coast.

That was too much. The United States at last declared war on Great Britain. Since it couldn't attack England directly, it determined to give the British a bloody nose by invading its colony, Canada.

To former President Thomas Jefferson, that seemed "a mere matter of marching." Surely, the United States, with a population of eight million, could easily defeat a mere three hundred thousand Canadians!

The odds, however, weren't quite as unequal as Jefferson supposed. Great Britain had 17,000 regular troops stationed in Upper and Lower Canada. The entire U.S. regular army numbered only 7,000, many of them badly trained.

Moreover, the British controlled the water routes – Lakes Huron, Erie and Ontario, and also the St. Lawrence River. For that was the key to both mobility and communication. The roads were almost worthless when they existed at all – not much more than rutted cart tracks. Everything – supplies, troops and weapons – moved by water.

When the war broke out, the Americans were prevented from using this water highway by the presence of the Royal Navy on the lakes. A British express canoe could move swiftly and fearlessly all the way to Lake Superior, carrying dispatches. But the American high command had difficulty communicating at all, which explains why its outposts didn't know for a month that the war was on. The Americans had to use express riders – bold men on horseback, plunging through a jungle of forest and swamp and exposed at every turn to an Indian ambush.

No wonder, then, that almost from the outset the War of 1812 developed into a shipbuilding contest, with both sides feverishly hammering men-of-war to completion in a race to control the lakes.

The Indians were another asset for the British. The

Americans had turned them into enemies, burning their crops and villages and hunting them down like wild animals. In American eyes, the Indians were an obstruction to be pushed aside or eliminated as the pioneers and settlers moved resolutely westward. But the Canadians hadn't fought the Indians since the days of the French-English wars fifty years before. They saw them as harvesters of furs, or, as in the case of the Mohawks of the Grand Valley, loyal subjects of the King.

The American attitude caused John Richardson's boyhood friend, Tecumseh, to move into Upper Canada from the U.S. with his followers to fight on the British side. The native allies numbered no more than 2,000 in all, but with their woodcraft they made a formidable enemy. The Americans were terrified of the Indians. The mere hint that a force of natives was advancing could send a chill through the blood of the citizen soldiers of Ohio or Kentucky.

As a member of the regular army, John Richardson wore a scarlet uniform and carried a musket almost as tall as himself. This awkward, muzzle-loading "Brown Bess" was the basic infantry weapon – and a notoriously inaccurate one. The little one-ounce (.03 kg) ball, wobbling down the smooth barrel, could fly off in any direction. Richardson and his fellow soldiers didn't bother to aim their weapons; they pointed them in the direction of the enemy, waited for the command, and then fired in unison.

The effect of several hundred men, marching in line and in step, shoulders touching, and advancing behind a spray of lead, could be devastating. The noise alone was terrifying. The musket's roar makes the crack of a modern rifle sound like a popgun. Smokeless powder was unknown; after the first volley the battlefield was shrouded in a thick fog of grey.

It required twelve separate movements to load and fire a musket. A well-drilled soldier could get off two or three shots a minute. By that time he was usually close enough to the enemy to rely on his bayonet.

Young Richardson learned to remove a paper cartridge from his pouch, tear off the top with his teeth, pour a little powder in the firing pan and the rest down the barrel. Then he stuffed it with wadding, tapped it tight with his ramrod and dropped in the ball. When he pulled the trigger it engaged the flintlock whose spark (he hoped) would ignite the powder in the pan and send a flash through a pinhole, exploding the charge in the barrel. As Richardson himself discovered at the Battle of Frenchtown later that year, it didn't always work. The phrase "a flash in the pan" comes down to us from those days.

Some of the American woodsmen used the famous Tennessee rifle, a far more accurate weapon because of the spiral groove inside the barrel. That put a spin on the ball – in the same way a pitcher does in baseball – making it far easier to hit the target. However, it was slower to load and was used mainly by snipers or individual soldiers.

A more terrible weapon was the cannon, which operated on the same flintlock principle as the musket. From the tiny three-pounders (1.4 kg)to the big twenty-four-pounders (eleven kg), these weapons were identified by the weight of shot they hurled at the ramparts of the defenders. A sixteen-pound (seven kg) ball of solid pig iron (known as "roundshot") could knock down a file of two dozen men. Bombs – hollowed out shot, crammed with powder and bric-a-brac, and fused to explode in mid-air – were even more devastating. Every soldier feared the canister and grape shot – sacks or metal canisters filled with musket balls that broke apart in the air, sending scores of projectiles whirling above the enemy.

Crude as they seem to us now, these weapons caused a dreadful havoc for the soldiers who fought in the war. Men with mangled limbs and jagged wounds faced searing pain because anaesthetics had not been invented. Yet, grievously wounded men pleaded with army surgeons to amputate a wounded limb as quickly as possible for fear of gangrene. They swallowed a tot of rum or whisky, held a bullet ("biting the bullet") between their gritted teeth, and endured fearful agony as the knives and saws did their work.

Sanitation in the field was primitive, for science had not yet discovered that diseases were caused by germs. Measles, typhus, typhoid, influenza, and dysentery probably put more men out of action than the enemy. The universal remedy was liquor – a daily glass of strong Jamaica rum for the British, a quarter pint (0.2 L) of raw whisky for the Americans. In battle after battle, the combatants on both sides were at least half drunk. Hundreds of youths who had never touched hard liquor in their lives learned to stiffen their resolve through alcohol in the War of 1812.

These were civilian soldiers, members of the militia. In Canada, the Sedentary Militia, largely untrained, was available in times of crisis. Every fit male between 18 and 60 was required to serve in it when needed. Few had uniforms, and those who did were as tattered as beggars. Often they were sent home to their farms after a battle to be called up later.

Some signed up in the Incorporated Militia of Upper Canada for the duration of the war. These were young men inspired by patriotism, a sense of adventure, or the bounty of 80 dollars paid to every volunteer upon enlistment. In Lower Canada, a similar body of the Select Embodied Militia, composed of men between 18 and 25, was drawn by lot to serve for a minimum of two years. They were paid and trained as regular soldiers. In addition some regular units were also recruited in Canada, bearing such names as The Glengarry Fencibles or the Canadian Voltigeurs.

The American draftees and volunteers were engaged by the various states for shorter periods – as little as a month, as much as a year. Most refused to serve beyond that period; few were properly trained. Born of Revolution and dedicated to absolute democracy, the United States had decided against a large standing army. The citizen soldiers even elected their own officers – an awkward and not very efficient process, sneered at by the regulars. And they were recruited to fight *only* in defence of their country.

That caused a major problem for the United States.

Legally, the state militia didn't have to cross the border. Hundreds who had been drafted reluctantly used that excuse when their superiors tried to goad them into attacking Canada. Jefferson had said it was "a mere matter of marching", but when the armies reached the border, the marching stopped.

They didn't want to fight any more than their former compatriots, now tilling the fields and tending the orchards on the other side. That was one of the reasons why this peculiar war ended in stalemate. The Americans derived very little benefit from it; nor did the Indians, who were eventually betrayed by both sides when the peace talks were held. The only real victors were the Canadians, who got no territory but gained something less tangible, yet in the end more precious. Having helped to hurl back five American armies, the plain people who had once been so indifferent to the war developed both a sense of pride and a sense of community. They had come through the fire and they had survived. In a very real sense the War of 1812 marked the first faint stirrings of a united Canadian nation.

Chapter One

The reluctant general

Like John Richardson, George Stephen Benjamin Jarvis was only fifteen years old when the War of 1812 broke out, but that didn't stop him from rushing to join the army. His family were fierce Loyalists who, after the American Revolution, had exchanged their comfortable home in Danbury, Connecticut, for the wilds of New Brunswick, and later the muddy roadways of Little York, the future site of Toronto.

As Loyalists, the members of the sprawling Jarvis clan were eager to do battle with their former compatriots. An older cousin, Samuel Peter Jarvis, was a member of a militia unit, the 3rd York Volunteers, but young George opted for the regular army and was accepted as a "gentleman volunteer" in the British 49th. That was the favourite regiment of Canada's leading military figure, Major-General Isaac Brock, who had once been its colonel. As a result, George Jarvis would shortly find himself in the thick of battle, splendid in the scarlet tunic and brass buttons of a professional warrior.

He was to take part in many memorable battles. Within two years, he would be put in charge of a company of more than one hundred men, most of them older than himself. But no moment would be quite as memorable as his first engagement when, on a soft autumn day, he dashed up the slopes of Queenston Heights right behind General Brock himself.

That battle, on October 13, 1812, was the most important ever fought on Canadian soil. There, on a high cliff overlooking the Niagara River, Canada successfully fought off an invasion by a formidable American army. She also lost her most famous military figure, whose death is commemorated by a marble pillar overlooking the battle ground.

Tourists travel by the thousands each summer to gaze on Brock's Monument and to follow the battle itself, its course marked by signs and plaques. The slopes up which George Jarvis and his fellow soldiers toiled and struggled are no longer red with the blood of the participants. In October, the bright leaves of the sugar maple form an orange carpet, as they did on that day so long ago, when two neighbouring countries found themselves locked in combat.

The unnecessary war belongs to history; it never should have happened. But it did give history a nudge: it helped create a sense of community among the settlers north of the border, many of whom were new arrivals. In a very real sense, the victory at Queenston Heights, renowned now in song and story, marked the beginning of a new nationalism. Having forestalled a common enemy, the young volunteers and the newly-arrived farmers began to think of themselves as Canadians.

The irony is that the general in charge of the American troops across the Niagara River didn't want to go to war. Stephen Van Rensselaer was an aristocratic landowner from Upper New York State. An American militia man with no military experience, he was totally opposed to the whole idea of invading a neighbour. But in July of 1812, in one of the supreme ironies of a foolish and ironic conflict, he found himself a general, no less, in charge of an army of reluctant troops, ordered by his government to invade and seize Upper Canada. Thus it became for him a matter of honour that he prosecute the new war to the fullest, even at the risk of his own reputation.

His was one of two American armies that lay poised on the international border in the summer of 1812 with orders to strike at Canada. His men were camped at Lewiston, New York, on the Niagara River, directly across from the little village of Queenston. A second army, under General William Hull, was massed at Fort Detroit, directly across from the Upper Canadian village of Amherstburg.

In those days communications moved no faster than the speed of a trotting horse. Stephen Van Rensselaer had no way of knowing that General Hull's army had been decisively defeated on August 16 by a force of British and Canadians under General Isaac Brock and Indians under the great Shawnee war chief, Tecumseh. Terrified of an Indian massacre, Hull had surrendered Detroit and most of Michigan Territory without a fight. But nobody on the Niagara River or in the American capital of Washington was yet aware of this disaster.

And so, believing that Hull had been victorious and was now moving into Upper Canada, the Americans were urging Van Rensselaer to attack at once. They were under the impression that the Canadian stronghold at Fort Amherstburg had fallen and that the road to victory lay wide open. That was an illusion that Van Rensselaer himself did not share. But he had to follow orders.

He was supposed to be helping Hull by keeping the British and Canadians off balance. But that wasn't easy. The British controlled not only the far shore, but also the Niagara River itself and the two Great Lakes, Erie and Ontario. Van Rensselaer had fewer than a thousand men to guard a front of thirty-six miles (fifty-eight km). A third of that force was too ill to fight. None had been paid. His men lay in the open without tents or covering. Ammunition was low; there were scarcely ten rounds per soldier. There were no big guns, no gunners, no engineers, and scarcely any medical supplies.

Worse still, the state militia was refusing to fight on foreign soil – as was their right under the American constitution. When the general planned a daring raid to capture a British gunboat, only sixty-six of his four hundred men agreed to join the expedition.

If the troops were reluctant, their militia leaders were inexperienced. Brigadier-General William Wadsworth of the New York State Militia knew so little of war that he pleaded to be released from the assignment. Stephen Van Rensselaer himself had no campaign experience. Nor did he look much like a soldier with his pert and amiable Dutch features and his shock of white hair curled in the style of the day. A Harvard graduate, a millionaire farmer, and a supporter of worthy causes, he was seen as a political threat by his rival, the Republican governor of New York, who gave him the post to get him out of the way. Not the best method of choosing an army commander whose men depended on him for their lives!

He accepted on the condition that his cousin, Solomon, be appointed his aide-de-camp. For Lieutenant-Colonel Solomon Van Rensselaer was a skilled military tactician – a regular soldier until the century's turn and then adjutant general for the state of New York.

Unlike the general, his handsome cousin was "all formed for war." The description came from the general's friend, Major John Lovett, who with the two Van Rensselaers formed a tight little trio. Because they belonged to the opposition Federalist party in the state they could trust no other advice but their own.

Lovett, a confirmed letter writer, kept a careful record of everything that was happening on the frontier. The war, he thought, "was an Ominous Gathering of folly and madness." But he was prepared to fight.

He was a poet, a bon vivant, a lawyer by profession and an amateur politician – a restless man, always seeking

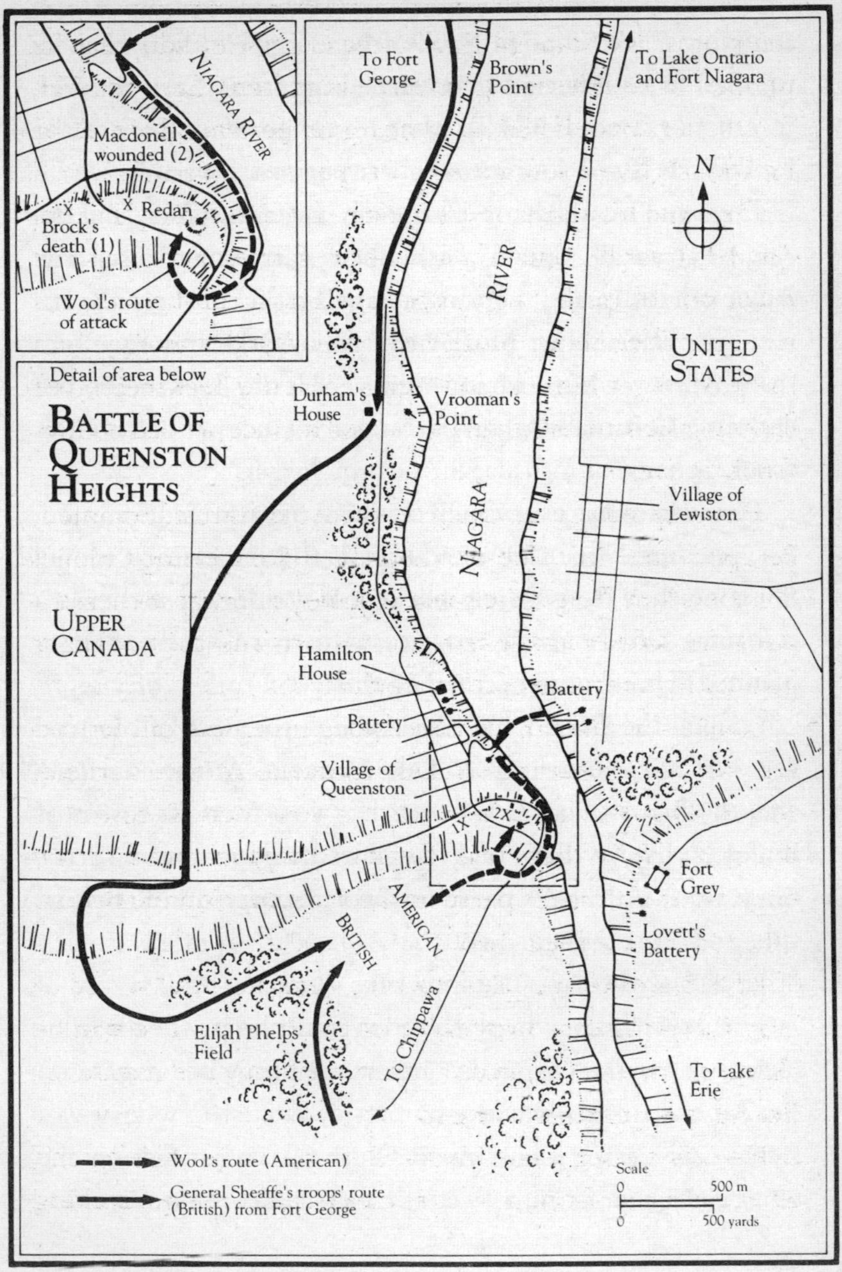

BATTLE OF QUEENSTON HEIGHTS
Detail of area below
Niagara River
Macdonell wounded (2)
Redan
Brock's death (1)
Wool's route of attack
To Fort George
Brown's Point
To Lake Ontario and Fort Niagara
N
Niagara River
United States
Durham's House
Vrooman's Point
Village of Lewiston
Upper Canada
Hamilton House
Battery
Battery
Village of Queenston
1X
2X
American
British
Fort Grey
Lovett's Battery
Elijah Phelps' Field
To Chippawa
To Lake Erie
Wool's route (American)
General Sheaffe's troops' route (British) from Fort George
Scale
0
500 m
0
500 yards

something new, changing jobs frequently. He didn't expect to become a soldier and he warned his friend, the general, "I am not a soldier." To that, Stephen Van Rensselaer replied, "It is not your *sword*, but your *pen* I want."

The Americans feared an early British attack, but on August 16 a red-coated British officer, galloping through the American camp and carrying a flag of truce, brought excitement and then relief. More riders followed, bringing letters from Albany where Major-General Henry Dearborn, the Supreme Commander, had arranged a truce with the Governor General of Canada, Sir George Prevost.

That was what everybody on the American side wanted. A truce, however brief, would allow the Americans to buy the time they desperately needed. It would allow them to reinforce the Niagara frontier, which was badly undermanned. That frontier stretched thirty-six miles (fifty-eight km) along the river, which cut through the neck of the land separating Lake Erie from Lake Ontario. At the southern end, the British Fort Erie faced the two American towns of Buffalo, a lively village of five hundred, and its trading rival, Black Rock. At the northern end, Fort George on the British side and Fort Niagara on the American bristled at each other across the entrance into Lake Ontario.

The great falls, whose thunder could be heard for kilometres, lay at the mid-point. Below the gorge of Niagara on the American side was the hamlet of Lewiston where Van Rensselaer's army was camped. On the Canadian side lay the village of Queenston, a partially fortified community overshadowed physically by the heights to the south and economically by the village of Newark (later Niagara-On-The-Lake) on the outskirts of Fort George.

At Lewiston the river was so narrow you could row across in ten minutes. A musket ball fired from one village to the other had the power to kill. For some time the Americans were convinced that the British would attack across the river. It was widely believed they had three thousand men in the field and another thousand on call. As is so often the case in war, both sides overestimated the forces opposite them.

General Isaac Brock had only four hundred regulars and eight hundred militia, most of whom had gone home to attend to the harvest. But New York state was totally unprepared for war. The arms were of varying calibres; no single cartridge would suit them. Few bayonets were available. There was only enough ammunition for one hour of fighting. The United States was not then the military machine it was to become in the twentieth century. Great Britain had the armed might.

Buffalo was in a state of panic. If Hull was beaten at Detroit only a miracle could save Rensselaer's forces from ignoble defeat. Now, when least expected, the miracle had happened. The army had been given breathing space.

Lieutenant-Colonel Solomon Van Rensselaer, an old campaigner, immediately grasped the significance of the armistice. However, he faced a serious problem: all the heavy cannon and supplies he needed were far away at Oswego at the eastern end of Lake Ontario. The roads were bogs. Supplies could only be moved by water. The British controlled the lake and, under the terms of the truce, would not allow the Americans to use it. Solomon, however, was determined to force his enemies to give way. The security of the American army depended upon it.

He went straight to his cousin, the general. Something would have to be done, he said. "I shall make powerful effort to procure the use of the waters and I shall take such ground as will make it impossible for me to recede."

"Van, you may as well give up, you will not succeed," his friend Lovett told him.

"If I do not, it will not be my fault," retorted Solomon.

He put on full military dress and crossed to Fort George. There he met Brock's deputy, Major-General Roger Sheaffe. But when he proposed the use of all navigable waters as a common highway, Sheaffe rapped out one curt word. "Inadmissible!" he cried.

Now Solomon decided to engage in a Yankee bluff. "There can be no armistice," he said; "our negotiation is at an end. General Van Rensselaer will take the responsibility on himself to prevent your detaching troops from this district." The British officers leapt to their feet. Sheaffe gripped the handle of his sword.

"Sir," said he, "you take the high ground!" His opponent also rose to his feet and gripped his sword.

"I do, sir, and will maintain it."

There was silence. Sheaffe paced the room and finally he

asked to be excused. Returning a few moments later after a discussion with his aides, he granted Solomon Van Rensselaer the use of the waters.

That was an enormous mistake. For it allowed the Americans to rearm themselves with the munitions stored at Oswego.

The truce could be cancelled by either side on four days' notice. It ended on September 8 with the Americans standing firm. Unless the British stopped their practice of seizing American ships and impressing American sailors, the Americans would continue the war. But by that time Van Rensselaer's army had been reinforced from Oswego with six regiments of regulars, five of militia, a battalion of riflemen – some six thousand men altogether – plus a great many heavy cannons and a quantity of pork and flour.

And so the balance of power on Lake Ontario had been tilted. General Van Rensselaer, taking advantage of the truce, shot off an express to Ogdensburg on the St. Lawrence to send nine ships to Sackets Harbor (near present day Watertown, New York). This move would aid the American navy in their planned attack on the Upper Canadian capital of York the following year.

In spite of this, Solomon Van Rensselaer was not a happy man. He felt himself the plaything of remorseless fate – surrounded by political enemies, forced into a war he could not condone, nudged toward a battle he felt he could not win, separated from a loving wife at his estate, 700 miles (1000 km) to the east. He knew communications were primitive, mail sporadic, dispatch riders scarce. Still, he fretted. Why had she not written? He had sent her a dozen letters and got no answer. He did not know – and wouldn't know until the affair at Queenston was over – that his wife Harriet was in the final stages of pregnancy and about to present him with a new son.

Chapter Two
Brock's frustration

Isaac Brock, returning home across Lake Ontario to his capital at York, was a national hero. He could not contain his ecstasy over his bloodless victory at Detroit, but even he was a little stunned by the wave of adulation that swept over the country – at the 21-gun salutes, the popular demonstrations, the gushy notes of congratulation. They were calling him the Saviour of Upper Canada; but Upper Canada was still in peril.

At 42, Brock was everybody's idea of a British warrior general – a handsome, strapping figure, standing six foot three (two m), magnificent in his scarlet uniform and gold epaulettes. Equally at home in ballroom or barracks, unmarried but much sought after by his female admirers, he was nothing if not bold and impetuous.

Now he was eager to follow up his victory and keep up the momentum against the invading Americans. He was ready to roll up the entire New York frontier and hammer at them while they were still off balance and poorly supplied. He wanted a quick victory – one that would allow him

to leave the stifling colonial atmosphere of Canada and get back to Europe to serve under the Duke of Wellington in the larger war against Napoleon.

But that was not to be. A message from Sir George Prevost informed him of the armistice the Governor General had concluded with the enemy. Prevost was hoping to conclude the war by a negotiated settlement without any more blood being spilled.

Brock had little patience with that. But his hands were tied and he could not conceal his bitterness. He was convinced that the sharp Yankees were using the armistice to buy time to reinforce their own position – and he was right. He must get back at once to Fort George on the Niagara frontier.

There he learned – from one of his officers who had been in Albany, New York, to arrange the armistice – that the Americans were convinced the British were weak. Certainly the Americans were stronger. He was dismayed to find how heavily they had been reinforced during the brief peace. He expected an immediate attack and sent at once to Amherstburg and Kingston for more troops.

There was one bright spot – the result, again, of the victory at Detroit. Three hundred Mohawk Indians were on the Niagara and another two hundred on their way under the controversial John Norton of the Indian Department. Born a Scotsman, now an adopted Mohawk chief, Norton saw himself as the successor to the great Joseph Brant.

Brock had mixed feelings about Norton's followers who

had cast aside their neutrality only as a result of British victories. To him any form of neutrality was little short of treason. He couldn't forgive the Mohawk. He couldn't understand why they didn't wish to fight for the British. He couldn't grasp the truth, that the quarrel was not really theirs and its outcome could not help them.

Brock wrote of "the disgrace into which they have fallen by their late conduct", but it is doubtful the Indians felt any sense of disgrace. They had simply been following a foreign policy of their own, which was to reap the benefits of fighting on the winning side.

Brock was eager to attack across the Niagara River and make himself master of upper New York state, but Prevost had reined him in. The Governor General still believed the path to peace lay in being as inoffensive as possible to the enemy. Even after the armistice ended he clung to the wistful fancy that the Americans would come to terms only if the British did nothing to annoy them. That was a foolish assumption. American honour had been stained; nothing would satisfy it but blood. It was psychologically impossible for the Americans to break off the war after the humiliation of Detroit.

Sir George Prevost made one telling point. Since the British were not interested in waging a campaign of conquest against the United States, but only in *containing* the war while battling the real enemy, Napoleon, it made sense to let the enemy take the offensive.

Brock had not been a soldier for the best part of three

decades without learning to obey orders. Frustrated or not, he did as he was told. While he believed he could sweep everything before him from Fort Niagara to Buffalo, he was prepared to let the Americans make the first move.

Certainly they did not appear ready for that. Many of their soldiers, tired of the army, were deserting to Canada. More, Brock believed, would do so if the opportunity were offered. Those deserters who did not drown in the swirling Niagara River reported a poor state of morale on the American side. They complained of bad food, poor pay, and continual sickness. They were jealous of the militia, which they believed to be better fed and better treated. Brock was scornful of the American militia. He saw them as an undisciplined rabble of "enraged Democrats . . . who . . . die very fast."

Brock did not have the temperament for the kind of bloodless warfare that had been his lot since hostilities began. He was impatient for action. Since he couldn't start it, he hoped and expected the Americans would. He was convinced they would have to make a move soon to keep their restless and undisciplined militia in line – and he was again correct. To warn of attack he'd ordered a line of beacon signals along the frontier. Now he could only sit and wait.

Actually the war in Canada was only a minor fracas. Who in Europe could take it seriously? On September 9, the day after Prevost's armistice ended, Napoleon launched and won the Battle of Borodino, thus opening his way to Moscow. On that day the casualties exceeded eighty thousand – a figure greater than the entire population of Upper Canada. Meanwhile, on the Niagara frontier, two tiny, untrained armies faced each other across the boiling river, each afraid to make the first move, each expecting the other to launch an attack.

Brock was certain something decisive would happen before the end of September: "I say decisive because if I should be beaten, the province is inevitably gone; and should I be victorious, I do not imagine the gentry from the other side will be anxious to return to the charge."

In short, he would either be confirmed as the Saviour of Upper Canada or there would be no Upper Canada. Whatever happened, Brock was convinced this brief and not very bloody war would come to a swift conclusion. There were, of course, other possibilities, glorious and at the same time tragic, but these he did not consider.

Chapter Three

Honour must be satisfied

In Lewiston, while Brock planned a defensive battle, General Stephen Van Rensselaer felt boxed in. He found himself pushed to the brink of a conflict for which he was inadequately prepared by a series of circumstances over which he had little control. Events began to pile up, one upon the other, like ocean breakers, driving him unwittingly towards a foreign shore.

On August 27, the camp was subjected to a dreadful spectacle. Across the river for more than a half a mile the men could see the remnants of Hull's defeated armies straggling along the opposite shore – ragged, shoeless, dispirited, the wounded groaning in open carts, the whole prodded onward by their British captors.

As Lovett put it in a letter to a friend: "The sensations this scene produced in our camp were inexpressible. Mortification, indignation, fearful apprehension, suspicion, jealousy, dismay, rage, madness." The effect on the American force was twofold: the militia was cowed by this demonstration of

British power. But the hawks among the officers yearned for action.

"Alarm pervades the country and distrust among the troops," General Van Rensselaer wrote. Like Hull's beaten soldiers, many of his own had no shoes. All were clamouring for pay. "While we are thus growing daily weaker, our enemy is growing stronger." The British were reinforcing the high ground above Queenston, bringing men and guns and fortifying every prominent point from Fort Erie to Fort George.

The day before the armistice ended, Major Lovett came to the conclusion that "we must either fight or run." Yet nobody on the American side could guess Brock's intentions or even estimate the true strength of his force, because not a single man could be persuaded to risk his neck by acting as a spy on the Canadian shore. Van Rensselaer had to resort to the time-worn trick of sending officers across under flags of truce to deal with the enemy on various pretexts while peering at the fortifications.

Meanwhile, at Albany, Major-General Dearborn, Van Rensselaer's superior, felt his resolve wavering. He had expected to seize all of Upper Canada, and Montreal as well, before winter. Now, Hull's defeat had shaken him. He was an old man, indecisive, inexperienced, out of his depth, peevish, uninformed and grossly overweight. The American military effort was in a state of confusion. Hampered by lack of supplies, men and money, he told the Secretary of War that he had never found official duties "so unceasing, perplexing and fatiguing as at this place."

Political enmities created further distractions. The quartermaster-general of the army, Peter B. Porter, was a political rival of the Van Rensselaers. He was organizing a whispering campaign against them, insinuating that the general was a traitor who intended to surrender his army the moment it crossed the river.

The general, however, was convinced that the British were about to attack and was preparing for them. He decided to maintain Fort Niagara, opposite Fort George at the mouth of the river, decrepit though it was, by removing the roof from a stone building, mounting two twelve-pound (five kg) cannon in its upper storey, and three big eighteen-pounders (eight kg) a kilometre upriver across from the British. He brought up an additional five hundred men stationed at Buffalo to strengthen his own force.

The British were also active. Gazing across the narrow river, Stephen Van Rensselaer could see the *Royal George* arrive with two hundred gunners. He had learned that one hundred smaller boats, loaded with stores for the British fort, had passed up the St. Lawrence together with two regiments of troops. The situation was critical. His plan was to hold out against what he thought to be superior strength until he was reinforced. There is no evidence that he contemplated an attack. It was the British who would attack – or so he believed.

But the British did not attack and the promised reinforcements did not arrive. In the American army of two thousand on September 22, 149 were too sick to fight, including

Solomon Van Rensselaer. The weather was dreadful. Raw winds and cold rains harassed the troops, soaking whatever blankets and tents were available.

In Albany, the capital of New York, General Dearborn continued to promise that money, men, and provisions would eventually be there. Troops were on their way from the western frontier to relieve Detroit, he said. But everything depended on what happened on the Niagara River: "*We must calculate on possessing Upper Canada before winter sets in*," Dearborn wrote, underlining that passage as if, by a stroke of the pen, he could will his ragtag army into victory.

To the relief of Van Rensselaer, the longed-for reinforcements arrived at the end of September. These included seventeen hundred soldiers under the command of one of the more curious specimens of American generalship, Brigadier-General Alexander Smyth. Pompous, self-important, and reluctant to follow orders, Smyth was a regular officer who disdained the militia. He had no intention of cooperating with his nominal commander, Van Rensselaer. Though he knew nothing of the country and had only just arrived, he advised the general that the best place for crossing the Niagara would be above the falls and not below them. As a result, he decided not to take his troops to Lewiston but to encamp them near Buffalo, thus splitting the American force. Nor did he report personally to Van Rensselaer. He claimed he was too busy.

By this time Van Rensselaer was determined to start

operations himself, since the British showed no interest in attacking. Dearborn had demanded action. For better or for worse, Stephen Van Rensselaer was determined that he should have it.

On paper his chances of success were excellent. He now had eight thousand troops under his command, half of them regulars. Forty-two hundred were encamped at Lewiston. The rest were at Buffalo or Fort Niagara. To counter this force, Brock had about a thousand regular troops, some six hundred militia, and a reserve of perhaps six hundred militia and Indians strung out thinly from Fort Erie to Fort George.

But numbers didn't tell the whole story. Morale, sickness, discipline, determination – all these Van Rensselaer must consider carefully. By his own count he had only seventeen hundred *effective* militiamen with him at Lewiston. The state of his army was such that he knew he would have to act swiftly if he acted at all:

"Our best troops are raw, many of them dejected by the distress their families suffer by their absence, and many have not necessary clothing. We are in a cold country, the season is far advanced and unusually inclement; we are half deluged by rain. The blow must be struck soon or all the toil and expense of the campaign will go for nothing, and worse than nothing, for the whole will be tinged with dishonour."

The key word was "dishonour". It crept like a fog through the sodden tents of the army, blinding all to reality. It hung like a weight over the council chambers in Albany and

Washington. Van Rensselaer felt its pressure spurring him to action, *any* action. No purpose now in disputing the war and its causes. No sense in further recriminations, or I-told-you-so's. Detroit must be avenged!

"The national character is degraded, and the disgrace will remain, corroding the public feeling and spirit until another campaign, unless it be instantly wiped out by a brilliant close of this." He knew that with his present force at Lewiston it would be rash to attempt an attack. But Smyth had arrived with an almost equal number, and that was enough.

Van Rensselaer planned a two-pronged attack: Smyth's regulars would cross the river near Newark (now Niagara-on-the-Lake) and storm Fort George from the rear. At the same time he would lead the militia from Lewiston to carry the heights above Queenston. That would divide the thinly spread British forces and cut their lines of communication, while driving their shipping out of the mouth of the Niagara River. It would provide the troops with warm and extensive winter quarters, act as a springboard for the following season's campaign, and – certainly not least – "wipe away part of the score of our past disgrace."

It was a workable scheme, but it depended upon Smyth's cooperation, and Smyth had no intention of cooperating. He acted almost as if Van Rensselaer didn't exist. When Van Rensselaer invited him to a council of officers to plan the attack, Smyth didn't reply. Even after Van Rensselaer wrote again, more explicitly, he didn't answer. Several days passed. Nothing. A fellow officer now informed Van Rensselaer that he had seen Smyth, who was unable to name the day when he could come to Lewiston for a council. The general thereupon sent a direct order to bring his command "with all possible dispatch." Silence.

This was a remarkable – almost unbelievable – state of affairs. In no other army would such defiance be tolerated, but the United States was not yet a military nation. The amiable Van Rensselaer didn't court martial his disobedient underling. He simply proceeded without him. He had told Dearborn that it would be rash to attack Queenston with the militiamen under his command at Lewiston. And yet, in spite of the fact that Smyth's regulars were out of the picture, he determined to do just that.

He had very little choice, because at this point an incident occurred near Black Rock close to Buffalo that reduced his options.

There, on October 9, a combined force of some hundred American seamen and soldiers managed to seize and put out of action two British gunboats, the *Detroit* and the *Caledonia*. They captured four cannon, two hundred muskets and so much pork that the British at Fort Amherstburg on the Detroit river were forced to live on half rations. They also captured a good many British soldiers.

This bold adventure represented the only American victory so far on the frontier. Its success goaded the Americans into premature attack. A thrill ran through the nation. At Lewiston, General Van Rensselaer was presented with an ultimatum from his troops who were now hot for action – or claimed to be. The general was warned if he didn't take the offensive immediately they would all go home.

With Smyth sulking in Buffalo, Van Rensselaer decided to abandon his two-pronged attack and launch a single assault upon Queenston. A friend in Albany counselled caution, but the time was long past when he could accept such cool advice. The pressure on him was so great that he realized that "my refusal to act might involve me in suspicion and the service in disgrace." As John Lovett described it, "he was absolutely compelled to go to battle, or reap such consequences as no man could endure." It was not possible to wait, even though there was no proper plan of attack. Ready or not, he would have to strike the blow at once.

CHAPTER FOUR
The attack begins

ON THE EVENING of October 11, 1812, at Fort George, Brock received an alarming note. Captain James Dennis, commanding a company of the 49th at Queenston, reported that his troops were in a state of mutiny and that the men had threatened to shoot their officers.

Brock at once dispatched Major Thomas Evans to seize the mutineers. "I will make an example of them," he said, by which he meant that they would all be executed by a firing squad.

At the same time Brock told Evans to cross the river and offer Van Rensselaer an immediate exchange of prisoners taken on the *Detroit* and the *Caledonia* for an equal number of Americans he had released after the capture of Detroit.

And so, on the very eve of the most famous battle on Canadian soil, a British officer was able to enter and have a good look at the enemy camp.

Evans reached Queenston the following night to find the guardhouse gutted and Dennis in a state of alarm. Just as he was about to arrest the ringleaders for mutiny he heard a scatter of musket fire from the American shore. Dennis told him that sporadic firing had been going on for some days, making it hazardous to use the door of the house on the river side of the building.

In spite of this hazard, Evans decided to cross the river at once and ordered Dennis to corral the prisoners for his return. Then, with shots still hurtling past his ears, he walked over to the home of a militia captain, Thomas Dickson, and asked his wife for a white handkerchief to use as a flag of truce while he and Dickson crossed the river. Mrs. Dickson protested. Others in the house joined her. They thought the venture far too dangerous. The enemy was in a temper. Evans was told they would no longer respect the white flag.

At that, Evans seized Dickson by one hand, took the flag in the other, descended the steep steps to a canoe at the water's edge, and started off across the two hundred yard (180 m) stream in a shower of musket balls. The canoe became unmanageable and was about to sink, when the American fire suddenly stopped and the two men were able to reach the far shore.

As Evans was about to leap ashore, an American with a bayonet stopped him. He asked to see the adjutant general, Solomon Van Rensselaer, but was told that Solomon was too ill to receive him. He replied that he carried an important message from Brock. Eventually Major Lovett appeared and Evans presented his request about the prisoner exchange.

Lovett's reply was abrupt and curiously evasive. He said nothing could be done "till the day after tomorrow."

This put Evans on the alert. What were the Americans planning for the next day? When he pressed his case, Lovett remained evasive. It appeared to Evans that Lovett was trying to delay his return to the Canadian side – it was already past mid-day. Lovett didn't come back for two hours and then explained the prisoners had been sent on to Albany and couldn't quickly be brought back. But, he said, "all will be settled the day after tomorrow."

That constant harping on the morrow confirmed Evans's suspicions that the enemy was planning an immediate attack. He was anxious to get away and report to Brock. He had kept his eyes open. He noticed the Americans' numbers had been "prodigiously swelled by a horde of half-savage troops from Kentucky, Ohio, and Tennessee." Even more significant, he spotted about a dozen boats half-hidden along the river bank and partially covered with brush. That convinced him "an attack on our shores could not be prudently delayed for a single day."

He and Dickson paddled swiftly back to their own shore. Evans rushed to warn the regular companies and the militia stationed at Queenston. It was now past three o'clock. Fort George was six miles (10 km) away. Every man would be needed to defend the town, including the mutinous prisoners who Evans liberated, appealing to their loyalty and courage.

Then, after making sure a fresh supply of ammunition had been distributed, the harried brigade major set off at a gallop for Fort George, warning the various posts along the route of the coming danger. He reached the fort at six, having been exposed for thirteen hours to "wet feet and extreme heat without refreshment of any kind." He was so exhausted he couldn't speak. He took some food, recovered his breath, and was ushered into the dining room before Brock and his senior officers.

They didn't believe him at first. They offered to place bets against his prediction of an attack on the following day. Even Brock appeared doubtful, but he changed his mind as Evans talked on. With a grave face he asked Evans to follow him into his office where he questioned him carefully on the day's events. At last he was convinced.

The two men came back to the dining room where the general issued orders calling out all the militia in the neighbourhood that very evening. Others in outlying districts were told to report as swiftly as possible. He returned to his office to work late into the night. Evans toiled until eleven making all necessary preparations to meet the coming assault. Then he slumped onto a mattress. A few hours later his slumber was disturbed by the rumble of distant guns.

The attack began at three o'clock in the morning of October 13, but General Stephen Van Rensselaer's plan and his preparations for the assault were both faulty. He had already lost the advantage of surprise. Now he decided to make the first crossing with only a handful of bateaux – two large boats, each holding eighty men, and a dozen smaller ones, each holding twenty-five.

Now the general's lack of military experience worked against him. His initial attack force, which would cross in two waves, consisted of some six hundred men, half of them militia. A few kilometres upriver were more boats that could easily be floated down, but the general didn't take advantage of these. He believed that, once the boats were emptied on the opposite shore, they could quickly return for reinforcements. He thought that half a dozen trips would be able to ferry the entire force across the river. That was a serious miscalculation.

He didn't think either to make use of the seamen at Black Rock. These men were experienced boatmen. His own militia, of course, knew the river well. They'd been staring at it and sometimes navigating it under flags of truce for some six weeks, but those who had just joined his force from Buffalo, Black Rock, and Fort Niagara were strangers to the area.

There were other problems. Van Rensselaer had failed to distribute enough ammunition. He had not insisted strongly enough on the use of Smyth's regular forces at Buffalo. Nobody had thought to find boats large enough to transport heavy field pieces across the river. The bateaux couldn't handle cannon. Nor had the various commands been assigned to capture specific objectives. The orders were general and vague: get across, seize the village, gain the heights.

It was still dark when the first boats pushed off in the teeth of a chill, sleety drizzle. To oppose the landing, the British had fewer than three hundred men in and about Queenston. But the defenders were on the alert. John Lovett, who had been placed in charge of the American battery at Fort Grey on the heights above Lewiston, noted that the Canadian shore was a constant blaze of musket fire.

He saw his friend Solomon Van Rensselaer land in what seemed to be a sheet of fire. His own eighteen-pound guns opened up to cover the attack, aided by two six-pounders (3 kg) and a mortar on the Lewiston shore. The cannonballs and shells whistled over the heads of the troops in the bateaux. But at the same moment, the British opened fire. Halfway up the heights in an arrow-shaped emplacement known as a *redan*, a single cannon began to lob eighteen-pound balls down on the boats. Darkness was banished as bombs burst and muskets flashed.

In one of the boats approaching the shore sat the oldest volunteer in the American army – an extraordinary Kentucky frontiersman named Samuel Stubbs, whose colourful turn of phrase enlivens his personal account of the battle. Sixty-two years old, scarcely five feet (1.5 m) in height, he gripped the rifle with which in just three months he had killed forty-five deer. Peering into gloom, illuminated now by the flash of cannon, Stubbs saw the opposite shore lined with redcoats "as thick as bees upon a sugar maple." In a few moments he was ashore under a heavy fire, "the damned redcoats cutting us up like slain venison," his companions dropping "like wild pigeons," while the musket balls whistled around him "like a northwest wind through a dry cane break."

Chaos reigned. Solomon's attack force had dwindled. Three of the boats, including the two largest containing almost two hundred men, had drifted downriver and turned back. On the bank above, Captain Dennis with forty-six British regulars and a handful of militia was keeping up a withering fire.

Solomon was no sooner out of his boat when a ball struck him in the right thigh. As he thrust forward, waving on his men, a second ball entered his thigh. The British were purposely firing low to inflict maximum damage. As the Colonel continued to stumble forward, a third penetrated his calf and a fourth mangled his heel. Still he didn't stop. Two more struck him in the leg and thigh. Weak from loss of blood, his men pinned down by the killing fire, he tottered back with a remnant of his force to the shelter of the steep bank above the river and looked around weakly for his fellow commander.

Where was Lieutenant-Colonel John Chrystie? He was supposed to be in charge of the regulars. But Chrystie was nowhere to be seen.

Chrystie's boat had lost an oarlock and was drifting helplessly downstream while one of his officers attempted to hold an oar in place. None of these regulars was familiar with the river. They all depended upon a pilot to guide them. But as they came under musket fire from the Canadian bank, the pilot, groaning in terror, turned about and returned to the American side. Chrystie, wounded in the hand by grapeshot, struggled with him to no avail. The boat landed on the American side several hundred metres below the embarkation point, to which Chrystie and the others would have to return on foot.

That was probably the turning point of the battle. Chrystie's problems and the heavy fire from the opposite shore "damped the hitherto irrepressible ardour of the militia," in Solomon Van Rensselaer's later words. The very men who the previous day were so eager to do battle – hoping, perhaps, that a quick victory would allow them to return to their homes – now remembered that they were not required to fight on foreign soil. They seized on any excuse to give up. One militia major suddenly lost his zest for combat and discovered he was too ill to lead his detachment across the river.

Back at the embarkation point, Chrystie found chaos. No one, apparently, had been put in charge of directing the boats or the boatmen, most of whom had forsaken their duty. Some were already returning without orders or permission, landing wherever convenient and leaving the boats where they touched the shore. Others were leaping into bateaux of their own and crossing over, then abandoning the craft to drift downriver.

As Chrystie struggled to collect the missing bateaux, his

fellow commander, Lieutenant-Colonel Fenwick, in charge of the second assault wave, arrived only to learn that he couldn't cross because there were no boats. Exposed to a spray of grape canister shot, he herded his men back into the shelter of the ravine until he managed to secure enough craft to move the second wave onto the river.

The crossing was a disaster. Lieutenant John Ball of the British 49th directed the fire of one of his little three-pounders, known as "grasshoppers", against the bateaux. One was knocked out of the water with a loss of fifteen men. Three others, holding some eighty men, drifted into a hollow just below the stone house built by Robert Hamilton, the best-known trader on the Frontier. All were slaughtered or taken prisoner, Fenwick among them. Terribly wounded in the eye, the right side, and the thigh, he counted nine additional bullet holes in his cloak.

None of the regular commanders had yet been able to cross the narrow Niagara. On the Canadian shore under the sheltering bank, Solomon Van Rensselaer, growing weaker from his wounds, attempted to rally his followers. They were still pinned down by cannon fire from the gun in the redan and the muskets of Captain Dennis's small force on the bank above.

But Captain John E. Wool, a young regular officer with the 13th Infantry, had a plan. He approached Solomon. Unless something was done and done quickly, he pointed out, all would be prisoners. The key to victory or defeat was the gun in redan. It *must* be seized. Its capture would signal a turning point in the battle that would relieve the attackers while the fire could be redirected, with dreadful effect, among the defenders.

But how could it be silenced? The heights were known to be unscalable from the river side. Or were they? Young Captain Wool had heard of a fisherman's path upriver leading to the heights above the gun emplacement. He believed he could bring an attacking force up the slope and asked Solomon Van Rensselaer's permission to attempt the feat.

He was just twenty-three years old – lithe, light youth of little experience but considerable ambition. One day he would be a general. The fact that he had been shot through the buttocks didn't dampen his enthusiasm. With his bleeding commander's permission, he set off with sixty men and officers, moving undetected through a screen of bushes below the river bank. Solomon's last order to him was to shoot the first man in the company who tried to turn tail.

As Wool departed, the Colonel slumped to the ground, among a pile of dead and wounded, a borrowed greatcoat concealing the seriousness of his injuries from his wet and shivering force. Shortly after that he was evacuated.

Meanwhile, Wool found the path and gazed up at the heights rising almost vertically more than three hundred feet (ninety m) above him. Creased by gullies, blocked by projecting ledges of shale and sandstone, tangled with shrubs, vines, trees and roots clinging to the clefts, they looked forbidding. But the Americans managed to claw their way to the top.

Wool, with his buttocks still smarting from his embarrassing wound, looked about him. Before him stretched an empty plateau, bordered by maples and basswood. But where were the British? Their shelters were deserted. Then, to his right, below, half-hidden by a screen of yellowing foliage he saw a flash of scarlet and realized that the gun in the redan was guarded by the merest handful of regulars.

Brock had brought his men down to reinforce the village – an error that would cost him dearly. Wool's men, gazing down at the red-coated figures manning the big gun, could not fail to see the tall officer with the cocked hat in their midst. It was the general himself. A few minutes later, when all his men were assembled, their young commander gave the order to charge.

CHAPTER FIVE

"Revenge the General!"

AT FORT GEORGE, Brock had been awakened in the dark by the distant booming of cannon. What was happening? Was it a feint near Queenston or a major attack? He was inclined to believe the first, for he had anticipated Van Rensselaer's original strategy to launch a two-pronged attack and didn't know about Smyth's obstinacy.

He was up in a moment, dressed, and on his grey horse Alfred, dashing out the main gate, waiting for no one, not even for his two aides, who were hurriedly pulling on their boots. On this dark morning, with the wind gusting sleet into his face and the southern sky lit by flashes of cannon, he did not intend to stop for anybody.

As he hurried through the mud toward Queenston, he met young Samuel Jarvis, a subaltern in his favourite militia unit, the York Volunteers. Jarvis, cousin of George, was galloping so fast in the opposite direction that he could not stop in time. But he finally reigned in his horse, wheeled about, and told the general the enemy had landed in force at the main Queenston dock. Jarvis's mission shouldn't have been necessary because of Brock's system of signal fires, but in the heat of battle nobody had remembered to light them.

On Brock galloped in the pre-dawn murk, past harvested grain fields, soft meadows, and luxuriant orchards, the trees still heavy with fruit. The York Volunteers, stationed at Brown's Point, were already moving towards Queenston. Brock dashed by, waving them on. A few minutes later his two aides also galloped by.

Dawn was breaking, a few red streaks tinting the sullen storm clouds, a fog rising from the hissing river as Brock, spattered with mud from boots to collar, galloped through Queenston to the cheers of the men of his old regiment, the 49th, including young George Jarvis. The village consisted of about twenty scattered houses separated by orchards, small gardens, stone walls, and snake fences. Above hung the brooding escarpment, the shore of a prehistoric glacial lake. Brock did not slacken his pace but spurred Alfred up the incline to the redan, where eight gunners were sweating over their eighteen-pounder.

From this vantage point the general had an overview of the engagement. Below him stretched the panorama of Niagara – one of the world's natural wonders, now half-obscured by the black smoke of musket and cannon. Directly below him he could see Captain Dennis's small force pinning down the Americans crouching under the riverbank at the landing dock. Enemy shells were pouring into the village from John Lovett's battery on the Lewiston heights, but Dennis was holding. A company of light infantry occupied the crest directly above the redan.

Unable to see Wool's men scaling the cliffs, Brock ordered the infantry down into the village to reinforce Dennis. Across the swirling river, at the rear of the village of Lewiston, he glimpsed battalion upon battalion of American troops in reserve. On the American shore several regiments were preparing to embark. At last Brock realized that this was no feint.

He instantly sent messages to Fort George and to Chippawa asking for reinforcements. Some of the shells from the eighteen-pounder in the redan were exploding short of their targets and he told one of the gunners to use a longer fuse. And then as he did so, the General heard a ragged cheer from the unguarded crest above, and looking up, saw Wool's men charging down upon him, bayonets glittering in the wan light of dawn.

He and the gunners had time for one swift action: they hammered a ramrod into the touch-hole of the eighteen-pounder and broke it off, thus effectively spiking it. Then, leading Alfred by the neck reins – for he had no time to remount – the Commander-in-Chief and the Administrator of Upper Canada scuttled ingloriously down the hillside with this men.

In an instant the odds had changed. Until Wool's surprise attack, the British were in charge of the battle. Dennis had taken one hundred and fifty prisoners. The gun in the redan was playing havoc with the enemy. Brock's forces controlled the heights. But now Dennis was retreating to the village and Wool's band was being reinforced by a steady stream of Americans.

Brock took shelter at the far end of the town in the garden of the Hamilton house. It would have been prudent, no doubt, to wait for reinforcements – but Brock was not prudent. As he saw it, hesitation would lose the battle. Once the Americans consolidated their position in the village and on the heights, they would be impossible to dislodge.

It was that that spurred him on to renewed action – the conviction that he must counterattack while the enemy was still off balance. Brock believed that whoever controlled the heights controlled Upper Canada. They could dominate the river and turn it into an American waterway. Possession of the high ground and the village would slice the thin British forces in two, give the Americans warm winter quarters, and allow them to build up their invading army for the spring campaign. In short, if Queenston Heights was lost, then the province was lost.

Brock managed to rally some two hundred men from the 49th and the militia. "Follow me, boys," he cried as he wheeled his horse back toward the foot of the ridge. He reached a stone wall and took cover behind it. Young George Jarvis, standing a few metres away, watched him dismount.

"Take a breath, boys," he said, "you will need it in a few moments." Jarvis and the others cheered.

He had stripped the village of its defenders, including

Captain Dennis, bleeding from several wounds, but still on his feet. He sent some men under Captain John Williams to attack Wool's left. Then he vaulted the stone fence and leading Albert by the bridle, headed up the slope at a fast pace, intent on taking the gun in the redan.

Jarvis and the others, struggling to keep up, slid and stumbled on the slippery footing of wet leaves. Above them, through the trees, Wool's men could be seen reinforcing the gun emplacement. A confused skirmish followed.

The battle seesawed. The Americans were driven almost to the lip of the precipice and somebody started to wave a white handkerchief. At that, Wool tore it away and ordered a charge. The British were beaten back.

The sun, emerging from the clouds, glistened on the crimson maples, on the Persian carpet of yellow leaves, on the epaulettes of the tall general, sword in hand, rallying his men for a final charge. It made a gallant spectacle: the Saviour of Upper Canada, brilliant in his scarlet coat, buttons gleaming, plumed hat, marking him unmistakably as a leader, a gap opening up between him and his gasping followers.

Did he realize he was a target? No doubt he did. He had already been shot in the hand. But that was a matter of indifference. Leaders in Brock's army were supposed to lead. The spectacle of England's greatest hero, Horatio Nelson, standing boldly on deck in full dress uniform, was still green in British memory. Both officers by their actions were marked for spectacular death; in fact they seemed to court it. Brock's nemesis stepped out from behind a clump of bushes and when the General was thirty paces from him, drew a bead with his long border rifle and buried a bullet in his chest, the hole equidistant from the two rows of gilt buttons on the crimson tunic.

Fifteen-year-old George Jarvis, only a few feet behind, ran up. "Are you much hurt, sir?" he asked. There was no reply. Brock placed his hand on his breast and slowly sank down lifeless. A grisly spectacle followed as a cannonball sliced another soldier in two and the severed corpse fell upon the stricken commander.

The gallant charge had been futile. Brock's men retreated down the hill carrying their general's body, finding shelter at last under the stone wall of the Hamilton garden at the far end of the village. Here they were joined by two companies of York Volunteers – the same men whom Brock had passed on his gallop to Queenston.

Arriving on a dead run, these soldiers caught their breath as American cannon fire poured down upon them from the artillery post on the opposite heights. A cannon ball sliced off one man's leg, and skipped on, crippling another in the calf. Then, led by Lieutenant-Colonel John Macdonell, the dead general's young aide, the enlarged force made one more attempt to recapture the heights.

Impulsively, Macdonell decided to follow his late commander's example. Possessed of a brilliant legal mind, he had little experience in soldiering. He called for a second frontal attack on the redan and seventy volunteers followed him up the heights to join the remainder of the 49th under

Captain John Williams taking cover in the woods. Together the two officers formed up their men and prepared to attack.

"Charge them home and they cannot stand you!" cried Williams.

The men of the 49th, shouting, "Revenge the General!", swept forward. Wool, reinforced by several more men, was waiting for them.

As Macdonell on horseback waved his men on, his steed was struck by a musket ball, reared and wheeled about. Another ball struck Macdonell in the back, and he tumbled to the ground fatally wounded. Williams, on the right flank, also fell, half-scalped by a bullet. As Captain Cameron rushed forward to assist his fallen Colonel, a ball struck him in the elbow and he too dropped.

In terrible pain, Macdonell crawled toward his closest friend, Lieutenant Archibald McLean of the York Volunteers, crying, "Help me!" McLean attempted to lead him away and was hit by a ball in the thigh. Dismayed by these losses, the men fell back bringing their wounded with them. Dennis was bleeding from five wounds. Williams, horribly mangled, survived. But Macdonell was doomed.

Everything that Brock feared had happened. The Americans now occupied both the village and the heights and were sending over reinforcements, now that they had unopposed possession of the river. The British had retreated again to the outskirts of the village. All of the big guns, except for the one downstream at Vrooman's Point, had been silenced.

At ten o'clock on this dark October morning, Upper Canada lay in peril.

At that point all the American forces should have been across the river, but so many boats had been destroyed or abandoned that General Van Rensselaer was finding it difficult to reinforce his bridgehead. Actually he had no more than a thousand men on the Canadian side and of these, two hundred were useless. Stunned by their first experience of warfare, the untrained militiamen cowered beneath the bank. No power, it seemed, no exhortation to glory or country, no threat of punishment could move them.

The general crossed at noon with his captain of engineers whose job it was to help the troops on the heights. Unfortunately all the entrenching tools had been left at Lewiston. They never did arrive. So the general sent Lieutenant-Colonel Winfield Scott, a regular officer, to the top of the ridge to take over from the wounded Wool. Then he prepared to return to the American shore. As he did so, a rabble of American militiamen leaped into the boat with him.

Scott worked furiously with the engineers to prepare a defence of the high ground. He knew that British reinforcements were on their way from Chippawa and Fort George – an American-born militiaman had deserted with that information. Scott would like to attack the Chippawa force, cutting it off from the main army, but he didn't have enough men for the job and his little force was diminishing. Whole squads of militia were slinking away into the woods and the brush of the bluffs.

He realized his danger. Ammunition was running out. He had managed to get a six-pound gun across the river in a larger boat, but there were only a few rounds available for it. In the distance he could see a long column of red-coated regulars marching up the road from Fort George under Brock's successor, Major-General Roger Sheaffe.

He desperately needed to get the eighteen-pound cannon at the redan into action to protect his rear and cover the landing of the reinforcements his general had promised him. But Brock had spiked it so well that Scott's men couldn't drive or drill the ramrod out. Scott scrambled down the hillside to help but as he did so a terrifying sound pierced the air – it was the screaming war whoop of the Mohawks. They came swooping out of the woods and hurtling across the fields, brandishing their tomahawks, driving in Scott's advance guard and forcing the trembling troops back. Only Scott's presence and voice prevented a general rout. The cries of the Indians carried across the river and sent a chill through the militiamen on the far side.

At about the same time, two British guns opened up in the garden of the Hamilton house effectively preventing the river crossing. Now Scott realized his chance of getting reinforcements before the final battle were slim. He could see the men he needed – hundreds of them, even thousands – lined up on the far shore like spectators at a prize fight. But for all the good they could do him, they might as well have been back on their farms where most of them fervently wished they were.

General Van Rensselaer was helpless. He had promised reinforcements and ammunition to the defenders on the heights, but could supply neither. He had sent to Brigadier-General Smyth asking for more men, but Smyth had again refused. He couldn't budge the troops at the embarkation point. They had been milling about for some hours in the drizzle watching the boats return with terribly wounded men and sometimes with deserters, watching other boats founder in the frothing stream. Now, with the screams of the Indians echoing down from the heights, they had no stomach for battle.

Unable to budge them, Van Rensselaer sent a note to the heights: "I have passed through my camp; not a regiment, not a company is willing to join you. Save yourselves by a retreat if you can. Boats will be sent to receive you."

That promise was hollow. For the terrified boatmen refused to recross the river.

Chapter Six
Victory

EARLIER THAT MORNING at Newark, Captain James Crooks of the 1st Lincoln Militia, noting the weather was bad, decided to turn over and go back to sleep and let his subordinate handle the parade. But, just as he started to doze off, a knock came at the window and a guard reported the Yankees had crossed the river at Queenston.

Crooks leaped from his bed, pulled on his uniform, and ordered his men to form up. At the fort's gate he ran into the artillery commander, Captain William Holcroft, who told him he was about to open fire on Fort Niagara across the river but was short of men. Crooks supplied him with several including Solomon Vrooman, who was sent to man the twenty-four-pounder (eleven kg) on a point almost two kilometres away. That big gun was never out of action and did incalculable damage. Indeed it was one of the reasons the American militia were refusing to cross the river.

A deafening artillery battery followed. The Americans heated their cannonballs until they glowed red and fired them into the village and the fort. They burned the court-

house, the jail, and fifteen other buildings before their batteries were reduced by the British cannon.

Meanwhile Brock's express had arrived from Queenston with orders for 130 militiamen to march immediately to the relief of the heights. Crooks assembled men from five companies, formed them into a reinforcement detachment, and marched them toward the scene of the battle. A kilometre out of Newark he was told of Brock's death. He tried in vain to keep the news from his men, but was surprised to find it had little immediate effect.

At Brown's Point, he passed one of the York Volunteers, who asked him where he was going. "To Queenston," he said. The officer told him he was mad. He said if he went any farther all his people would be taken prisoner. The general was dead. His force was completely routed. His aide was mortally wounded. Four hundred Yankees were on his flank, moving through the woods to attack Newark. Crooks dismissed all this, replying that he had his orders and would keep going. He told his men to load their muskets and marched on. Shortly after that he encountered a second officer who repeated almost word for word what he had heard a few minutes before. Again, Crooks ignored him.

About a kilometre from town he halted his men at a farm house. It was filled with American and British wounded, including the dying Macdonell. The troops were hungry, having missed their breakfast. Crooks sent them foraging in a nearby garden to dig potatoes. Soon every pot and kettle in the house was bubbling on the fire, but before the potatoes could be eaten General Sheaffe arrived with the remainder of the 41st Regiment and ordered them to fall in. Off they marched to battle, still hungry.

Sheaffe was a cautious commander. He had no intention of repeating Brock's frontal assault. He planned instead a wide flanking movement to reach the plateau above the village, where Wool's Americans were preparing for battle. His force would veer off to the right, away from the river, before entering the village, make a half circle around the heights, and climb under cover of the forest by way of an old road two miles (3.2 km) west of Queenston.

Here Sheaffe expected to be joined by the second detachment that Brock had ordered from Chippawa. In this way he could keep his line of march out of range of the American guns on the heights above Lewiston. At the same time, the Indians who had preceded him would act as a screen to prevent the enemy patrols from intercepting him as he formed up for battle.

Meanwhile, Captain Holcroft of the Royal Artillery had at great risk managed to trundle two light guns through the village, across the ravine, and into the garden of the Hamilton house. He was guided by Alexander Hamilton himself, a local merchant, son of the original owner, who knew every corner of the ground. It was these guns that Winfield Scott heard, effectively blocking the river passage, as John Norton and his Mohawks harassed his forward positions.

The Indians, screening Sheaffe's force, continued to harry the Americans. They poured out of the woods, whooping and firing their muskets. Then they vanished into the trees, preventing Scott from consolidating his position and driving in the advance guard and flank patrols to prevent contact with the advancing British. Bit by bit they were forcing the Americans into a tighter position on the heights.

Their nominal chief was John Brant, the eighteen-year-old son of the late Joseph Brant, the greatest of the Mohawk chieftains. But the real leader was the theatrical Norton, a strapping six-foot (two m) Scot who thought of himself as an Indian and had ambitions to succeed his late mentor. He was more Indian than most Indians and had convinced many British leaders that he was a Cherokee. He wore his black hair in a long tail held in place by a scarlet handkerchief into which he had stuck an ostrich feather. Now, brandishing a tomahawk, his face painted for battle, he whooped his way through the woods, terrifying the American militia and confusing the regulars.

Directly behind the woods on the brow of the heights, hidden by the scarlet foliage and protected by the Mohawks, Roger Sheaffe formed up his troops. He was in no hurry. He controlled the road to Chippawa and was waiting for Captain Richard Bullock to join him with another one hundred and fifty men from the south.

Captain Dennis of the 49th had already joined his company, his body caked with blood. Exhausted and wounded as a result of the battle at the river's edge, he refused to leave the field until the day was won. Now he stood with others, waiting for the order to advance, while the American gunners poured down fire from across the river. For the unblooded militia, the next hour was the longest they had known as a rain of eighteen-pound balls and smaller shot dropped about them.

At about four o'clock, just as Bullock came up on the right flank, Sheaffe ordered his men to advance in line. He now had about a thousand men. The enemy had almost the same number. But many of the American militia, with the war cries of the Indians echoing in their ears, had fled into the woods or down the cliff and toward the river.

When Scott counted his dwindling band, he was shocked to discover that it numbered fewer than three hundred. In the distance he saw the scarlet line of British regulars, marching in perfect order, Indians in one flank, the militia slightly behind, two three-pound (1.4 kg) grasshopper guns firing. He had just received Van Rensselaer's despairing note that reinforcements were not possible. The Americans called a hurried council and agreed to a planned withdrawal.

Now the battle was joined. James Crooks, advancing with his militia detachment, had been in many hailstorms but none, he thought, wryly, where the stones flew as thick as bullets on this October afternoon. Little scenes illuminated the battle and remained with him for the rest of his days: the sight of an Indian tomahawking a York militia man in the belief that he was one of the enemy; the sight of the Americans' lone six-pounder (3 kg), abandoned; the bizarre spectacle of Captain Robert Runchey's platoon of black troops –

escaped slaves – advancing beside the Indians; the sight of a companion, his knuckles disabled by a musket ball at the very moment of pulling the trigger.

Scott's regulars were attempting to cover the American withdrawal. The colonel himself leaped on a fallen tree and literally made a stump speech, calling on his men to die with their muskets in their hands to redeem the shame of Hull's surrender. But the British advance continued with all the precision of a parade-ground manoeuvre, which, of course, it was. The Americans were trapped between the cliff edge on their left and the cannon fire from Holcroft's gun in the village below them on their right.

The Indians whooped forward once more. The British and Canadian militia advanced behind with fixed bayonets. The American line wavered, then broke. The troops rushed towards the cliffs, some tumbling down the hill, clinging to bushes and outcroppings, others, crazed with fear, leaping to their deaths on the rocks below. Scores crowded the beaches under the shoulder of the mountain, waiting for boats that would never come. Others, badly mangled, drowned in the roaring river.

Winfield Scott, Wadsworth, and their fellow officers realized now that only a quick surrender would save their force from being butchered by the Indians. But the problem was how to get a truce party across to the British lines. Two couriers, each carrying a white flag, had tried. The Indians had killed them both. So Scott decided to go by himself.

There were no white handkerchiefs left. But the engineering officer had a white cravat, which Scott tied to his sword point. He would rely on his height and his splendid uniform to suggest authority. But these attributes were of little value because he was immediately attacked and seized by young Brant and another Indian who sprang from a covert and struggled with him. Scott's life was saved by the timely appearance of John Beverley Robinson and his friend, Samuel Jarvis of the York Volunteers, who freed him and escorted him to Sheaffe.

There the British general accepted Scott's surrender and called his bugle to sound the cease fire. The Mohawks paid no attention. Enraged at the death of two of their chiefs they were intent on exterminating all the Americans huddled under the cliff. Scott hotly demanded to be returned to share their fate, but Sheaffe persuaded him to have patience. He was himself appalled at the slaughter. After the battle was over some of his men would remember their general flinging off his hat, plunging his sword into the ground in a fury, and demand that his men halt the bloodshed or he, Sheaffe, would immediately give up his command and go home. A few minutes later the firing ceased, and the battle was over. It was half-past four. The struggle had raged for more than twelve hours.

Now, to Winfield Scott's humiliation and despair, some five hundred militia men appeared from hiding places in the crevices along the cliffs and raised their hands in surrender. The British had taken 925 prisoners, including a brigadier-general, five lieutenant-colonels, and sixty-seven other officers. They let one man go free – the little sexagenarian, Samuel Stubbs of Boonsboro, Kentucky. Stubbs had expected to be killed and scalped. Now he discovered that the British looked on him as an oddity – as if he had been born with two heads. A British officer took one look at him and let him go. "Old daddy," he said, "your age and odd appearance induce me to set you at liberty, return to your home and think no more of invading us!"

Stubbs promised cheerfully to give up fighting but he didn't mean it. "I was determined I wouldn't give up the chase so, but at 'um again." And so he was, all the way from the attack on Fort York to the bloody battle of New Orleans where, in his sixty-sixth year, he was responsible for the deaths of several British officers.

The Americans suffered some two hundred and fifty casualties, including the mangled Solomon Van Rensselaer, who would eventually recover, and John Lovett, who was incapacitated for life. What began as a lark for him ended as tragedy. For Lovett, the conversationalist and wit, the world went silent. Placed in charge of the big guns on the heights above Lewiston, he was rendered permanently deaf.

By contrast the British casualties were light. They had lost only fourteen killed and seventy-seven wounded. But there was one loss that could not be measured and by its nature evened the score at the Battle of Queenston Heights. Isaac Brock was gone, and there was no one to fill his shoes.

Chapter Seven

Brock's legacy

ALL OF CANADA was stunned by Brock's loss. His own soldiers of the 49th who were with him in Holland and at Copenhagen were prostrated by the news. Of all the scenes of sorrow and despair that day, the most emotional is the one reported by Lieutenant-Colonel Driscoll of the 100th Regiment who had come up from Fort Erie to help direct artillery fire against the American battery at Black Rock.

At two that afternoon Driscoll looked up to see a provincial dragoon gallop up, dishevelled, without sword or helmet, his horse bathed in foam, his own body spattered with mud.

One of Brock's veterans, a man named Clibborn, spoke up:

"Horse and man jaded, sir; depend upon it, he brings bad news."

Driscoll sent the veteran across to discover what message the dragoon had brought. The soldier doubled over to the rider but returned at a funereal pace, and Driscoll realized something dreadful had occurred. He called out:

"What news, Clibborn? What news, man? Speak out."

Clibborn walked slowly toward the battery, which was still maintaining a brisk fire at the Americans across the river. Musket balls ploughed into the ground around him. He didn't seem to see them. He couldn't speak, could only shake his head. At last, he slumped down on the gun platform, his features dead white, his face a mask of sorrow.

Driscoll couldn't stand the silence and shook Clibborn by the shoulder.

"For heaven's sake, tell us what you know!"

Clibborn answered at last, almost choking:

"The general is killed; the enemy has possession of Queenston Heights."

With those words, every man in the battery became paralyzed. Guns ceased firing. These men of the 49th, all of whom had served under Brock in Europe, were shattered by the news. Some wept openly, others mourned in silence, several began to curse in frustration. The sound of enemy cheers, drifting across the river, roused them to their duty. In a helpless rage over the death of their General, they became demonic, loading, traversing, firing the heavy guns as if they were light field pieces, flinging round after round across the river in an attempt to avenge their former chief.

All over the province, similar expressions of grief were manifest. Major Glegg, Brock's military aide, called it "a public calamity." Young George Ridout of the York Volunteers wrote his brother: "Were it not for the death of General Brock and Macdonell our victory would have been glorious . . . but in losing our man . . . is an irreparable loss."

Like many others, young Ridout was convinced that Brock was the only man capable of leading the divided province. Samuel Jarvis crossed the lake to bring the news of the tragedy where "the thrill of dismay . . . was something indescribable."

Sir George Prevost, when he learned of his general's death, was so badly shaken he could scarcely hold a pen with which to report the tragedy to his superiors.

Meanwhile, Sheaffe concluded an immediate armistice with the Americans, "the most ruinous policy that ever was or could have been adopted for the country," to quote a nineteen-year-old subaltern, William Hamilton Merritt, the future builder of the Welland Canal. Certainly had Brock lived, he would have pursued Van Rensselaer's badly shaken force across the river to attack Fort Niagara and seize the northern half of New York State. But Sheaffe was a more cautious commander.

Brock's body, brought back to Newark, lay in state for three days. His funeral, in George Ridout's words, was "the grandest and most solemn that I have ever witnessed or that has been seen in Upper Canada." Guns boomed every moment during the funeral procession while across the river at both Niagara and Lewiston the Americans fired a salute to their old enemy.

Upper Canada was numb, its people drawn closer by a common tragedy that few outsiders could comprehend. In the United States, attention was quickly diverted by another naval skirmish in which the American frigate *Wasp*, having disabled the captured British sloop of war *Frolic*, was herself taken by the enemy.

Europe was far more interested in the fate of Moscow under attack by Napoleon, who at that very moment was preparing to withdraw his army from the charred and deserted Russian capital. That bitter decision, still unknown to most of the world, marked the beginning of the end of the war with France. Had President Madison foreseen it, the invasion of Canada by the Americans, still scarcely underway, would never have been attempted.

The picture of Brock, storming the heights at Queenston, urging on the brave York Volunteers and saving Canada in the process, is one that would become part of an imperishable legend for the fledgling nation. He was the first Canadian war hero, an Englishman who hated the provincial confines of the Canadas, who looked with disdain on the civilian leaders, who despised democracy, the militia and the Indians, and who could hardly wait to shake the Canadian mud from his boots. None of that mattered. His monument stands today, dominating the ridge, not far from where he fell.

Here is where the myth of Isaac Brock began. By Confederation it had grown to the point that the battlefield had become, in the phrase of the *Canadian Monthly*, "one of Canada's sacred places." Yet, with Brock dead, Upper Canada – and Lower Canada too – would need more saviours. The war was not over – nor would it be for another two years.

Brock's splendid pillar has become a mecca for tourists, reinforcing the myth of Brock that began to grow within moments of his death. He is remembered less for his real contribution to the country: his military foresight, his careful preparation for war during the years of peace, his astonishing bloodless capture of Fort Detroit, an American stronghold. Today when Canadians hear his name, the picture that still forms in their minds is of that final impetuous dash, splendidly heroic but tragically foolish, up the slippery heights of Queenston on a gloomy October morning.

Index

Coming Soon

THE BATTLE OF LAKE ERIE

Pierre Berton returns to his series on the battles of the War of 1812 in this thrilling saga of men, muskets, cannons, and sailing ships. The great naval battle on Lake Erie in the summer of 1813 was fought by fifteen battleships – nine American, six British – each one of which had been constructed of timber felled on the shores of the lake. In *The Battle of Lake Erie*, Pierre Berton vividly illustrates how two brilliant commanders fought each other to a standstill – and how one turned crushing defeat into a brilliant victory.

THE DEATH OF TECUMSEH

The Shawnee chief Tecumseh was perhaps the greatest native leader in the War of 1812. Allied with the British, he was both feared and admired by his American foes. In September 1813 in what is now southwestern Ontario he fought to the death at the Battle of the Thames. To this day no one has been able to locate Tecumseh's grave, and both his death and life have become the stuff of legend.

Also Available

Jane Franklin's Obsession

Little did Lady Jane Franklin know that when her husband, Sir John, left England in 1845 to find the fabled North West Passage, she would never see him – or his crew – again.

By 1847, Lady Franklin was deeply worried about the fate of her husband and his two ships in the Arctic. They had seemingly disappeared without a trace. For the next eleven years, she pressed for a solution to this mystery. Expedition after expedition was sent forth, mapping previously uncharted waters and land masses enroute. When, in 1858, Lady Franklin finally knew the fate of her husband, it shocked the world – and gave birth to a legend.

Trapped in the Arctic

Few ideas gripped the minds of Victorian Age explorers more than that of the North West Passage. The belief that there was an all-water route from the Atlantic Ocean to the Pacific prompted dozens of ships and thousands of men to thread their way around the forbidding islands of Canada's Arctic in search of the elusive prize.

No Arctic explorer was braver or more ambitious than handsome Robert John McClure. That same ambition proved almost fatal in 1851-53 when McClure's ship was trapped in the ice at Mercy Bay and starvation threatened the lives of his crew.

In *Trapped in the Arctic,* Pierre Berton tells the exciting story of McClure's heroism and foolhardiness, and the combination of luck and courage that led him to claim discovery of the fabled North West Passage.

Also Available

The Men in Sheepskin Coats

As the nineteenth century gave way to the twentieth, the Canadian West experienced an unprecedented wave of immigration and settlement. Many of these homesteaders were "the men in sheepskin coats" and their families – natives of eastern Europe who had left their impoverished, crowded homelands for what they hoped would be a better life.

At first they were not welcomed with open arms. Politicians and newspaper writers spoke of them as "foreign trash." Gradually, however, these hard-working immigrants came to be seen as essential to Canadian prosperity and the idea of the Canadian mosaic.

In this second instalment of *Canada Moves West,* Pierre Berton vividly captures the hardships and triumphs of Canada's Slavic settlers as they struggle to find "a place in the sun" in the vastness of the West.

Steel Across the Plains

William Cornelius Van Horne was the greatest railway man in North America. As the energetic chairman of the Canadian Pacific Railway (CPR), it was his job to ensure that a ribbon of steel would be laid down between Winnipeg and Calgary in record time. It was an epic, back-breaking task, involving more than 7,000 men and 2,000 teams of horses and spanning 1,000 kilometres. By the end of 1883, the railroad was a reality on the prairie. Soon towns with names such as Moose Jaw and Swift Current were dotting the map.

In *Steel Across the Plains,* Pierre Berton vividly recreates the events that opened the West to white settlers — and signalled the end of the traditional native way of life.

Also Available

A Prairie Nightmare

Isaac Montgomery Barr was a Christian minister with a vision of settling western Canada with industrious Anglo-Saxon farm families. But were his ambitions entirely honourable?

In 1903 Barr brought 2,000 unsuspecting British colonists to what is now Saskatchewan and eastern Alberta. "Agriculture is simple," he had told them before they embarked. "The work is not very hard." But hard it most certainly was …

In the third instalment of *Canada Moves West,* Pierre Berton presents a lively recreation of the life and times of Isaac Barr, the false promises he made, and the hard lives his followers endured.

City of Gold

By the spring of 1898 Dawson had gone from being hardly a dot on the map to being the greatest boom-town in the world. Thousands walked its muddy streets and visited its rooming houses, theatres, saloons and gambling-halls. It was a city where a mug of milk would cost you five dollars and a broom fifteen.

Gold was what had lured most of these people to this Yukon outpost. And it would be gold, discovered 3000 km to the west in Alaska, that would seal Dawson's fate….

City of Gold is the fourth instalment of *The Great Klondike Gold Rush,* part of Pierre Berton's series *Adventures in Canadian History.*

Also Available

TRAILS OF '98

There was no single trail to the fabled riches of the Yukon's Klondike region. There were many. And all of them were difficult.

In *Trails of '98*, Pierre Berton vividly captures all the determination and folly, courage and foolhardiness of the would-be prospectors who crossed ocean, mountain, river, and glacier in search of gold. Some men spent two years on these trails. Of the thousands who took them, the vast majority never reached the longed-for Klondike at all!

Trails of '98 is the third volume in a series devoted to the frenzy for gold that gripped Canada's Yukon – and the world – between 1896 and 1899.

BEFORE THE GOLD RUSH

Before news of the great Klondike gold strike was heard around the world, several hundred fortune-seekers were already scrabbling for gold along creek banks in the Yukon and Alaska.

Cut off from the world, clustered in squalid log towns with no link to civilization except a small steamerboat that arrived once a year with provisions, these free-spirited individuals made their own laws, with the power to execute or banish anyone who broke them. Many were strange characters, men with names like Cutthroat Johnson and Jimmy the Pirate. And when gold was found on the Klondike, most became millionaires – if only for a few months.

Before the Gold Rush is another instalment in Pierre Berton's vivid history of the Klondike Gold Rush of the late 1890s.